LIST OF CONTENTS

OREP

EDITIONS

15, rue de Largerie - 14480 Cully
Tél. (33) 02 31 08 31 08
Fax : (33) 02 31 08 31 09
www.orep-pub.com
info@orep-pub.com

Publisher : Philippe PIQUE
Layout : Laurent SAND
Text by : Lieutenant Colonel Alain FERRAND
Photographs : The collection du Musée d'Arromanches and Philippe PIQUE
Models and maps : OREP
English translation : Heather Costil

Graphic conception : OREP
ISBN : 978-2-912925-08-4
Copyright OREP 1997
All rights reserved

Legal deposit : 1st term 2010
Printed in France

■ German gun battery at Longues sur Mer

The raid on Dieppe on 19th August 1942 confirmed the Allies in their view that the Atlantic Wall was heavily defended at those places favourable to landings, and particularly so in the area around the Channel ports.

The capture of a fortified position on the French coast would therefore be costly in human life and extremely difficult. To seize, intact, a port or harbour was a hope highly unlikely to be realized. Nevertheless, for an invasion to succeed, the Allies had an imperative need to acquire a means of landing and handling the tonnage of material and supplies required by a modern mechanised army, namely 40kg per man per day.

During the Quebec Conference in July 1943, the plans devised by the close collaboration of the British and American Chiefs of Staff for the Allied strategic operations in

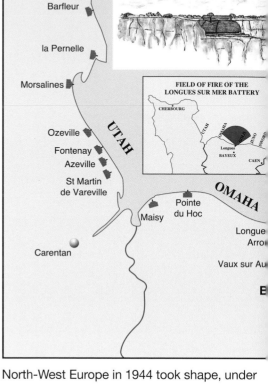

North-West Europe in 1944 took shape, under the code name OVERLORD. These plans were to achieve the largest combination of air, land and naval operations known to history, with the dual purpose of supporting the Soviet Army in its struggle against the Nazi forces and the liberation of Western Europe.

On the speed with which reinforcements and supplies could reach Normandy would depend the success of the landings and the remainder of the campaign. With the support of air and naval forces, it was going to be necessary to land, under enemy fire, large land forces and to supply these with the reinforcements, equipment, food, war materials and supplies essential, once a bridgehead had been established, so that they could break out and advance into the heart of Europe to destroy the enemy's forces.

■ German gun battery at Longues sur Mer

Sited about 6km west of Arromanches, the battery at ⦁ngues is an interesting example of coastal defences. Its field fire extended over large area of the bay of the Seine. Its four ⦁2 mm guns could hit a target some 20 km distant.

Situated about 350m from the gun emplacements and 65m ⦁ove sea level, on top of the cliffs, the command post compri-⦁d two floors.

In the lower floor, which was half-buried, was the observa-⦁n station, with a viewing slit extending over an arc of more ⦁n 180°.

The upper floor was protected by a concrete roof slab sup-⦁rted on four small steel columns and contained the range-fin-⦁g equipment needed to determine the distance of the target. ⦁e co-ordinates were transmitted to the gunners by telephone.

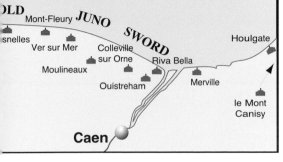

To supply the Allied forces continuously from points on the beaches would a high-risk ope-ration, because bad weather, if combined with adverse tides, could lead to disaster and inter-rupt the flow of supplies. It was therefore imperative to be able to land supplies without being subjected to such natural obstacles. The answer was to build a prefabricated port or harbour in England and to tow it across the Channel, install it in position and bring it into service with all possible speed.

To maintain an infantry division facing the enemy would require supplying it with 300 to 400 tonnes each day; an armoured division would need 1,200 tonnes. During the early stages of the invasion, given the size of the forces deployed, the supplies having to cross the Channel would amount to between 8,000 and 12,000 tonnes per day, without taking into account the need of the forces consolidating themselves in the bridgeheads. Following this phase, the daily requirements would grow, month by month, by between 1,000 and 2,000 tonnes.

During an amphibious operation, there is always a critical period when the initial waves of assault troops become tired. If the men of the follow-up and consolidation forces are not speedily on hand, or inadequate in strength or in supplies, this critical period may become extended and put in danger the success of the operation. This critical period starts on the second day of an operation.

Once the beaches had been won, the Allies needed quickly to reinforce their forces in the narrow beachhead, before Rommel's troops could reach the battlefield. Under these conditions, port facilities were essential for supplying of the land forces.

■ German gun battery at Longues sur Mer

THE NEED FOR PREFABRICATED HARBOURS

The initial objective of the landing was to secure a wide bridgehead comprising Brittany and a part of Normandy, from the Seine to the Loire and ending at a line from Rouen to Orleans, but not a pitched battle to end in the destruction of the German Army of the West. This latter objective would only be achieved during the second week of August, when the Allied armies trapped the Germans in the Falaise pocket.

During the first phase, from D-day to D-day + 17, the military plan envisaged taking Cherbourg and the Cotentin Peninsular and covering its Calvados flank to the east of Caen.

During the second phase, the Allies would hold Caen to guard their left flank and would then move from the Cotentin towards Rennes and Nantes, to isolate the Brittany peninsular. This operation was to be completed by the thirtieth day.

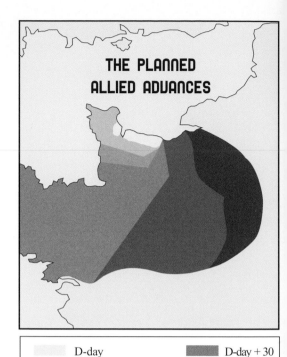

THE PLANNED ALLIED ADVANCES

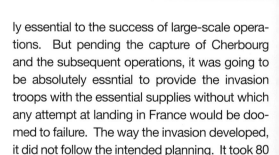

	D-day		D-day + 30
	D-day + 9 (postponed to D-day + 15)		D-day + 60
	D-day + 17		D-day + 90

The third phase was to last for two months and consisted of liberating the Brittany peninsular up to the Loire, organising a naval base in Quiberon Bay (Operation CHASTITY), then extending eastwards the Normandy bridgehead as far as the Seine, and to the South-East, up to the Nantes-Orleans line.

It was only to be at the end of three months that, based on this wide bridgehead, with the Allied armies reinforced, the British through Cherbourg and the Americans by a base to be created in Morbihan Bay, they would push to the East, towards the heart of Germany, ready for the decisive battle to end the War.

From the start, we can see the vital importance attached to ports, whose capture was clear-

ly essential to the success of large-scale operations. But pending the capture of Cherbourg and the subsequent operations, it was going to be absolutely essntial to provide the invasion troops with the essential supplies without which any attempt at landing in France would be doomed to failure. The way the invasion developed, it did not follow the intended planning. It took 80 days to reach the Seine and then 20 days in pursuit of the enemy before the front was stabilised. However, by the 12th of September, there remained no German combatants in Normandy (except for those taken prisoner).

Landing craft were intended to beach themselves on the shore and discharge men and war materials ; however, the Royal Navy considered that frequent beaching would damage the bottoms of these craft and that, therefore, this method of landing men and materials should be reserved for assault operations and not for supply missions. Moreover, beaching was a time-consuming operation because it was necessary to wait for the next favourable tide for the vessel to be refloated.

Furthermore, the number of troop landing craft (LCT), as well as their tonnage, was limited and the use of cargo ships and coasters thus appeared to be essential. But a 2,000 tonne ship cannot approach an open Normandy shore closer than 1 nautical mile. In addition, to speed up the turn-round and to achieve a continuous flow of supplies, it would be essential to unload these directly on the lorries that would transport the supplies to the troops.

THE ADVANCE OF THE ALLIED ARMIES

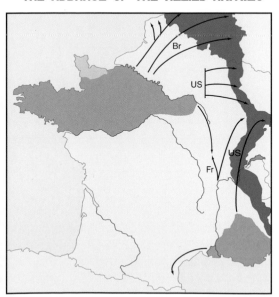

░░	Advance of the armies on D-day + 50
▒▒	Advance of the armies on D-day + 80
██	Advance of the armies on D-day + 100
→	Lines of advance of the allied armies

Finally, even if it were possible for troops to be landed relatively quickly from beached landing craft, to achieve the same efficiency in the offloading of vehicles and supplies required for the frontline troops, it would be necessary to have available quays and ship discharge facilities.

Under these circumstances, and given the absence of any certainty that an existing port could be seized by force, the construction of artificial port and harbour facilities became a matter of vital importance.

As early as 1941, Churchill had instructed Admiral Mountbatten to develop amphibious warfare techniques and to investigate the possibilities for installing unloading quays on beaches.

On 30th May 1942, the British Prime Minister wrote a memorandum to Mountbatten regarding the attractions of floating quays and jetties. Thereafter, in the greatest secrecy, a team under the designation « Transportation 5 » or « Tn.5 », was made responsible for designing port structures. Answers to the problems involved only began to emerge after Churchill started to take a personal interest in the subject, making it clear in a circular, later to became famous, that he would tolerate no delay (« Bring me the best solution; do not waste time talking about the problems, these will look after themselves »).

It was on the occasion of the « Rattle » Conference, held in Scotland on the 2nd and 3rd July 1943 that, for the first time, the Allies brought up the question of artificial harbours and port facilities

Later in the month, this subject was to be examined in greater detail during the Quebec

Conference, in the presence of Churchill and Roosevelt.

General Eisenhower, Commander in Chief of the Allied Forces and Admiral Sir B. Ramsay, commander of the Allied naval forces, took the view that until such time as existing French ports could be seized, the whole of OPERATION OVERLORD could not take place without the use of artificial ports.

To Vice-Admiral W. G. Tennant was designated the responsibility for all aspects of the artificial harbours. On D-day he had under his control more than 500 officers and around 10,000 men.

The harbour-creation project as a whole was given the code name « Mulberry ». This name was chosen at random, but later it was observed that mulberry trees grow rapidly in size, a happy omen for an enterprise which had speedily to be brought to fruition. The problem of speed of installation, off the beaches, was of the essence for these harbours. It was intended that their installation should be completed within two weeks and that they should have the capacity of the Port of Dover (Dover covered 310 hectares and, in 1944, would have allowed the discharge of 6,000 tonnes of supplies and 1,250 vehicles per day). However, its construction had taken seven years!

These harbours would serve a dual purpose:

- They would provide shelter for shipping and particularly for flat-bottomed vessels such as landing craft.
- They would ease the problems of landing troops, vehicles and supplies of all kinds.

In their initial studies, the planners had assumed the landing of an assault force of 3 Divisions, increased to 10 Divisions as from D-day+5 and followed by the landing of one Division per day. Under this scenario, some 10,000 tonnes per day would be required on D-day+3, 15,000 tonnes on D-day+12 and 18,000 on D-day+18. However, the alterations to the plan of attack, made by the Commander in Chief at the beginning of 1944, to increase the D-day assault force by two Divisions, substantially increased these forecast requirements.

Because of the problems that would be involved in towing across the Atlantic enormous sections of artificial harbour, it was decided that these harbour structures (Mulberry A for the Americans and Mulberry B for the British) would be built in Great Britain, despite the many problems this might cause, and be towed across the Channel.

Each harbour would consist of :

- An outer, floating, breakwater made up of « bombardons ».

- An inner, fixed, breakwater consisting of concrete caissons and of ships expressly scuttled for this purpose, together known as GOOSEBERRIES.

- Floating jetties, extending from the beaches to jettyheads, mounted on jack-up piles, against which ships could berth.

For technical reasons the concrete breakwater caissons could not be sunk in water deeper than 10 metres, but they would nevertheless enable coastal ships to use the inner harbour in calm water conditions whilst the larger vessels of the « Liberty Ship » type could unload in the rather less sheltered water behind the floating breakwaters.

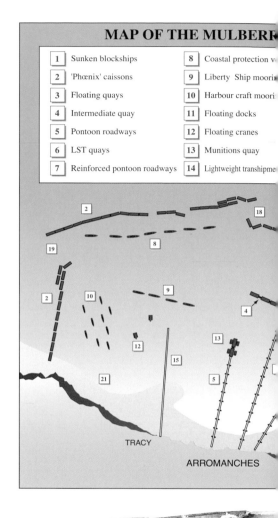

MAP OF THE MULBERR

1	Sunken blockships	8	Coastal protection v
2	'Phœnix' caissons	9	Liberty Ship moori
3	Floating quays	10	Harbour craft moori
4	Intermediate quay	11	Floating docks
5	Pontoon roadways	12	Floating cranes
6	LST quays	13	Munitions quay
7	Reinforced pontoon roadways	14	Lightweight transhipme

TRACY

ARROMANCHES

■ Floating roadways

■ Phoenix caissons

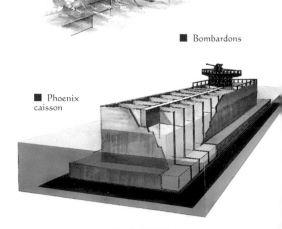

■ Bombardons

■ Phoenix caisson

OUR AT ARROMANCHES

15	Floating, fabric, roadway known as a 'Swiss Roll'
16	Small landing craft moorings
17	Eastern entrance
18	Northern entrance
19	Western entrance
20	Service vessels sheltered basin
21	Low tide line

Ponton piers

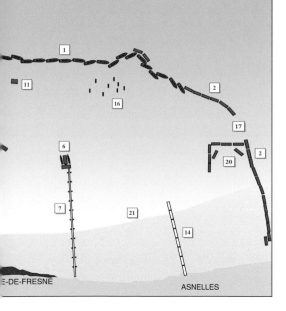

E-DE-FRESNE
ASNELLES

■ Floating Quay ▲   ■ Intermediate quay ▲

■ Floating roadways

It should be noted that high water mark traditionally denotes the line of demarcation between the responsibilities of the British Navy and Army and, in consequence, although the responsibility for constructing the caissons was a matter for the War Office, it was the Navy that was responsible for getting them into position.

In practice, it took a whole year to design and build all the elements making up the harbours. The task was a major one, and the personal intervention of Churchill became necessary to resolve all the problems and to determine the priorities. At a period when all the UK naval shipyards were fully occupied with building landing craft, special basins had to be excavated along the banks of the Thames in which the Phœnix caissons could be constructed.

By the 6th June, everything was ready. Whilst the ships which were to form the rings of blockships set sail, the other elements of the harbours were readied to be towed across the Channel by 132 tugs. The bombardons left first, followed, on the nights of the 6th and 7th June, by the Phœnix caissons.
While the story of this risky operation is unfolding, let us have a look at a harbour such as its designers envisaged it.

PRACTICAL PROBLEMS IN BRINGING THEM TO FRUITION

■ Blockships

Approaching from the open sea, we encounter successively:

THE ARTIFICIAL BREAKWATERS, OR « GOOSEBERRIES » :

Placed in position off the five invasion beaches (including those which would not comprise a « port »), in order to facilitate unloading operations, these were made up of floating elements, the "bombardons" and sunken elements, blockships, or, in addition, Phœnix caissons. They provided an area of sheltered water offshore of the beaches and thus allowed the berthing of landing craft and the unloading of shipping.

THE FLOATING BREAKWATER MADE UP OF « BOMBARDONS » :

Situated offshore of the artificial harbour structures, this first type of breakwater was composed of a chain of floating, cruciform-shaped, rafts. Each steel raft was 65m long, 8m high and had a draught of 6m. They were hollow, and could be partially filled with water, but remained afloat thanks to watertight compartments. They were anchored in 20m of water and each was separated from its neighbour by some 15 metres. Placed end to end, they constituted a barrier 1,600m long.

A bombardon is an application of a principle which had been discovered during the preliminary studies. It was found that when a wave hits a heavy, floating barrier, it loses a great deal of its energy. Thus, a 2 metre high wave is reduced to 1 metre in the lee of the barrier.

Protected by the bombardons from the heavier swells, large merchant ships, unable to discharge their cargos in the inner harbour, owing to their draught, could nevertheless acceptably transfer cargo to other suitable craft, DUKWs and RHINO-FERRIES. The latter, huge steel platforms, propelled by outboard

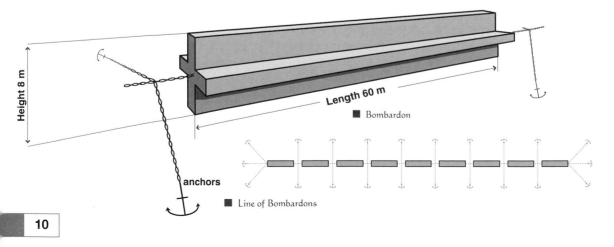

Height 8 m

Length 60 m

■ Bombardon

anchors

■ Line of Bombardons

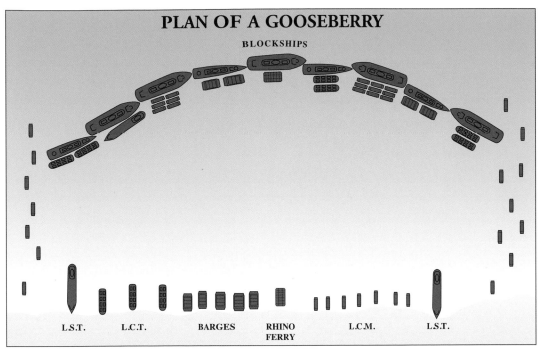

motors, were used to transport vehicles and armour between the ships and the beach. This type of raft weighed 400 tonnes and measured 60 m by 15 m. It was difficult to manoeuvre except in very calm seas. The freeboard was only 30 cm. A large number were lost during the storm of mid-June. The elements going to make them up could be transported vertically along the sides of LSTs and they could then be assembled, according to requirements.

■ Blockship

OLD VESSELS SCUTTLED TO CONSTITUTE « BLOCKSHIPS »

The fact of being able to sink old ships to form breakwaters was a considerable advantage in that the ships, being able to move into position under their own power, permitted a saving in tug resources, which were limited and for which there was an immense need, for towing the harbour elements across the Channel and for putting them into position, not to mention meeting the requirements of ports back in Britain.

Obsolete warships and merchant ships, the vessels chosen for scuttling on the 7th June, in front of the beaches and in a depth of 5 metres at low tide, were chosen so that their height from keel to upper deck was at least 40 feet; this meant that at high tide, a minimum of two metres would be above water. They would thus constitute a mole, or continuous protective wall for the artificial harbour lying within and provide sheltered water for the unloading operations which had to start at the earliest possible moment, without waiting for the harbour as a whole to become operational. They would also proved shelter for the smaller ships during high winds and storms.

In addition, it was realised that the upperworks of these ships could be used as administrative quarters, for first aid care, as repair shops and as living quarters for the crews of the barges ferrying supplies between the large ships anchored offshore and the beaches.

In all, these old vessels made up some 7,000 metres of breakwater spread among the five invasion beaches. Among them, the old French cruiser 'Courbet', scuttled off Sword beach, was able to render a last service to the Allies.

We should not overlook, in this short historical account, that on 7th June, at UTAH beach, the German coastal batteries were still operational, while the construction of the Gooseberry I was proceeding, and sank the second and third blockships. Nevertheless, happily, these went down in their intended positions, but Radio Berlin announced this as a success by the German defenders!

THE SHELTER-JETTIES, OR SUNKEN « PHŒNIX » CAISSONS

The initial demand was for 147 caissons for both harbours. 212 were constructed up to the summer of 1944. They served to strengthen the harbour sea defences or were later used to repair certain ports which had been destroyed, such as Le Havre, and the dykes at Walcheren in Holland.

Six different sizes were required, to take account of the sites where they were to be sunk (a task taking from 22 to 50 minutes depending on sea conditions and requiring continuous monitoring and improvement). The largest displaced 6,044 tonnes and the smallest 1,672 tonnes. The largest were 60 metres long, 17 metres wide and 18 metres high. The entire number required 275,000 cubic metres of concrete, weighing almost 600,000 tonnes, 31,000 tonnes of steel and a million and a half square metres of corrugated steel sheet. Each caisson took 4 months to construct.

Towed across the Channel by powerful tugs, the caissons were sunk in front of the shore

along the contour line of 9 metres at the deepest. They constituted the backbone of the breakwaters protecting the harbours and completed the chain of breakwaters made up of Gooseberries. Each caisson comprised, in addition to a shelter for the crew during transit, a platform for mounting a Bofors anti-aircraft gun, with protection for its crew, and finally, a hold for twenty tonnes of ammunition formed within the upper part of the structure. (Contrary to what is sometimes asserted, it would not appear that the caissons had served to hold carburants. No document relating to them makes any mention of this. One can see at least two good reasons why they should not have been used for this purpose; the caissons

could only be held in position on the seabed if they were filled with seawater or sand. Had they been filled with fuel oil or other fuels at the time the other ships were being loaded in Great-Britain, they would have become lighter and would have tended to float out of position, thus defeating their original purpose. Moreover, the caissons being open to the elements, rain and seawater would have contaminated the fuel, which would have caused problems.

The caissons sunk offshore had no decks. Others were sunk side by side at right angles to the shore, constituting shelter-jetties giving lateral protection to the harbour and serving as unloading quays for small ships.

« WHALE PIERS » OR « LOBNITZ PIERS » :

These berthing quays were concrete and steel pontoons of 1,100 tonnes deadweight. Rectangular in shape, they were fitted at each corner with square-section steel piles, 30m long and weighing 40 tonnes, and sliding in specially-designed housings. Vertical movement of the piles was controlled by cable and pulley systems powered by large diesel engines.

Thanks to this ingenious system, they were able to follow the rise and fall of the tides and continuous unloading of ships was therefore ensured, whatever the state of the tide. The interior of each structure comprised eighteen compartments, to provide technical services rooms, storage, and quarters for the crew. To increase the overall length of these quays, and their unloading capacity, intermediate concrete structures were sunk between adjacent floating structures.

In addition, a further refinement was incorporated in the floating quays, consisting of a sort of steel ramp which could be lowered slowly into the water. It was designed to allow the unloading of Landing Ship Tanks (LST). This system, to which was added a side platform, permitted simultaneous unloading from both decks of such vessels, so achieving a considerable saving of time. When an LCT was beached, the lower deck of the vessel was discharged first of all, then, by means of an internal hoist, the vehicles on the upper deck were brought down to the lower deck for unloading.

At the same time, on the other sides of the floating quay, it was possible to discharge the cargo from coastal vessels directly on to waiting lorries.

■ Floating roadways

■ Quays

FLOATING ROADWAYS FORMING JETTIES :

These were articulated steel structures designed to be mounted on steel or concrete caissons. At one end, they were fixed to the beach and at the other, to floating pontoons. Given the tidal range on this coast, the range of vertical movement of these elements could reach six metres whilst, at low water, the caissons rested on the sand. For both harbours, it was planned to provide a total of eleven kilometres of flexible roadways as well as a special anchoring system to prevent them from oscillating and breaking up under the influence of the tidal currents. Depending on their intended use, these roadways could support 25 or 40 tonne armoured vehicles.

Originally designed all to be built of steel, a material in very short supply at this period, many floaters (470 of a total of 670) were finally built of concrete. To do this, it was necessary to develop a concrete structure which was both strong and light, as well as being watertight and able to float. These floating structures were called « Beetles ». Half a dozen of them can still be found on Arromanches beach

Some steel caissons were employed in areas of rocky sea-bed where, close inshore, concrete caissons would have been damaged. They had incorporated in them, four small adjustable stilts.

During their transportation across the Channel, these structures were towed in lengths of 150m, but proved to be particularly vulnerable to the elements, 50% of them being lost.

ADAPTING THE BEACHES

It had to be possible to cross :
- the tidal belt of wet sand whose consistency varied from hour to hour.
- the belt of dry sand above high water mark, sometimes prolonged by dunes or cliffs in which breaches had been blown by the Allied bombardment.
- behind the dunes, or the cliffs, were marshy areas, or else a plateau with only rare roads or paths inadequate to take the heavy traffic envisaged.

Three types of materials for creating instant roadways were available :
- prefabricated interlocking perforated metal sheets called PSPs ; rolls of metal mesh of various shapes and strengths which could be unrolled and anchored to the ground (of which vestiges can still be found in the sand dunes at UTAH beach).

- A surfacing material consisting of rolls of a natural fibre, coconut or raffia, which could be laid by a modified tank known as a "BOBIN" (a punning name coined by the British General HOBART).
- a surfacing material consisting of a felt impregnated with bitumen and called « Prefabricated Bituminous Surfacing ».

THE REAR MAINTENANCE ZONE :

This zone was of capital importance for the British supply system. It was situated between the main base in Great Britain and the Army Corps maintenance areas. It occupied the whole zone to the south of Arromanches and the three British beaches, extending to the south of Bayeux and to the gates of Caen. Main roads linked this zone and the logistical units of the attacking forces.

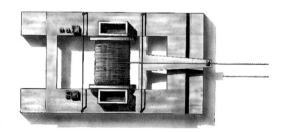

■ Cable reel for anchor cables for floating roadways

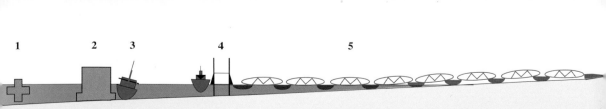

1 : Bombardons
2 : Phœnix caissons
3 : Blockships
4 : Quays
5 : Floating jetties

■ ■ ■ PRACTICAL PROBLEMS IN BRINGING THEM TO FRUITION

The various elements were constructed and assembled in ports along the South coast of England. The finished Phoenix caissons were filled with water and allowed to sink to the sandy seabed, in order to concal them from any Germans reconnaissance planes and to protect them while they were waiting to be transported across the Channel. On the eve of D-day, they were refloated by pumping out the water which had kept them on the sea bottom.

On 6th June, D-day, tugs towed the first elements of the artificial harbours towards the Normandy beaches. For their part, the ships destined to be scuttled to form GOOSEBERRIES had been made ready some hours earlier. They would arrive first and, from the 7th June, would form an initial sheltered area which would facilitate the landings on each invasion beach.

During the night of D-day/D-day+1, Admiral RAMSAY took a decision which was to have serious consequences at the time of the storm later in the month. To economise on tugs and on the manpower needed for other tasks, he decided to reduce the double line of bombardons, as originally proposed, to a single line. This would reduce the expected attenuation of the force of the swell. In addition, because of a mistake, the bombardons were deposited in water of twice the originally-planned depth.

On 8th June, the caissons arrived in sight of the beaches.

On 10th June, Mulberry A already comprised 6 scuttled ships forming an initial breakwater, but only two Phoenix caissons and twelve bombardons had been. anchored. This delay was due to enemy fire against the harbour area.

■ General view of the Mulberry harbour

At Mulberry B, the mole had been installed to the West of the North harbour entrance and a start had been made on the LST jetties. The work went on, night and day, under the protection of an artificial fog

On 11th June, the Gooseberries were in position on the Utah, Omaha, Gold, Juno and Sword beaches.

On the 17th of June, the chains of bombardons were all in position. At Arromanches, the East floating roadway of the future central quay had been in place since the 14th of June, with, at its extremity, a quay enabling coasters to unload directly onto supply lorries. The installation of the LST jetty was delayed, owing to the loss during transport of numerous sections of floating jetty, among which were numerous units fitted with adjustable corner jacks. At St. Laurent, a first unloading station and its access road was in service.

On 16th June, the central jetty of Mulberry A was finished and linked to the berthing quay. It appears that on this day the Germans finally understood the importance of the Mulberries and started to launch air attacks on them. They were defended by the Allied Air Forces and by anti-aircraft guns on the ships, the caissons themselves, and the beaches. Anti-aircraft balloons and smoke screens completed the defences.

■ Cable reel for anchor cables for floating roadways

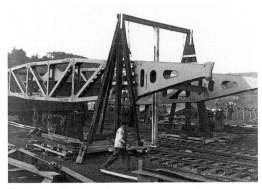

■ Installing floating roadways

■ Light vehicles being unloaded

On 17th June, the major part of the caissons which were to form the main breakwaters of the artificial harbours was in place off the Normandy coast and the bombardons had been anchored in their final positions. At Arromanches, with the consent of the Mayor, the German seafront defences which hindered the exits from the harbour were destroyed.

■ Installing floating roadways

At Mulberry A, the planned 24 bombardons had been anchored in position, 32 of the 51 Phoenix caissons were in place and moorings for two Liberty Ships were available. Three floating jetties were in the course of being completed and two of the six berthing quays on jack-up piles were installed.

The central quay, reserved for unloading LSTs, operated at the average rate of one LST per 64 minutes, that is to say, one vehicle every 1 minute 16 seconds (Instead of the 12 to 14 hours needed to unload and then wait for the next tide). Thereafter, all the troops landed at Omaha were able to do so with dry feet, across the floating roadway. The Plan had not envisaged Mulberry A being finished before the 24th June.

At this time, the harbour at Arromanches was much closer to being finished than that at ST. LAURENT, for the reason that the British had been able to carry out some assembly trials of the major elements at the end of May and the beginning of June, while the Americans were unable to do so, the elements having been delivered too late for this.

In each artificial harbour, 115 barges and RHINOs and 100 DUKWs were at work discharging the ships pending the installation of the floating quays that would enable direct unloading to take place.

The harbour at Arromanches already provided a safe shelter for the small craft such as DUKWs and RHINOs

■ Unloading platform

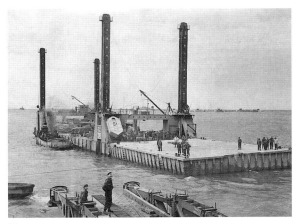
■ Installing loading platforms

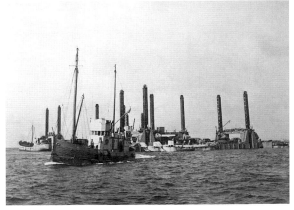
■ Towing unloading platforms

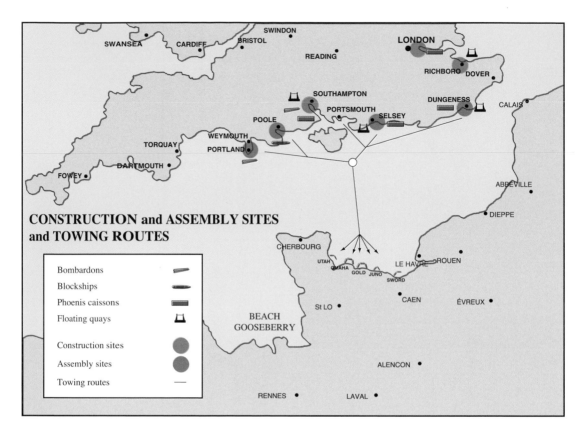

SWINDON
SWANSEA   CARDIFF   BRISTOL
READING
LONDON
RICHBORO DOVER
SOUTHAMPTON
PORTSMOUTH   DUNGENESS   CALAIS
POOLE   SELSEY
WEYMOUTH
TORQUAY   PORTLAND
DARTMOUTH
FOWEY
ABBEVILLE
DIEPPE

CONSTRUCTION and ASSEMBLY SITES and TOWING ROUTES

CHERBOURG
UTAH   ROUEN
OMAHA   LE HAVRE
GOLD JUNO
SWORD

Bombardons	
Blockships	
Phoenis caissons	
Floating quays	
Construction sites	
Assembly sites	
Towing routes	

BEACH GOOSEBERRY
St LO
CAEN   ÉVREUX
ALENCON
RENNES   LAVAL

which ensured the transportation of supplies between ship and shore .

Once completed, the harbour would provide :

- two floating quays, arranged in a T-shape and connected to land by a reinforced floating roadway for the landing of all vehicular equipment, (the east quay)
- seven floating quays and their intermediate elements, connected to land by two jetties and enabling unloading to take place in an endless stream (as well as the embarkation of the wounded), (the central quay)
- a special pontoon consisting of two floating quays linked together by a jetty and reserved solely for unloading munitions, (the west quay)

■ Construction of a platform

Phoenix caissons

Installing Phoenix caissons

The combination of the several types of breakwater enabled the harbour at OMAHA beach, Mulberry A, to make available the capacity to moor 7 Liberty Ships, 5 large coasters and 7 medium-sized coasters. Its 3 berthing quays and their floating jetty had a capacity of 40 tonnes for the one reserved for discharging tanks, and 25 tonnes for the other two.

There were 6 berthing quays, grouped in twos, and able to accept either LSTs or coasters, or both.

The port could thus unload a daily tonnage of 5,000 and 1,400 vehicles. In addition, a floating roadway connected to the shore enables LCTs and other landing craft (LCT = Landing Craft Tanks, of which there were 9 types, capable of transporting 3 to 8 heavy tanks or 250 to 300 tonnes of supplies) to unload directly from their holds.

Only four Phoenix caissons were lost during the installation phase, two by bad weather, one by hitting a mine, and the other, hit by a torpedo.

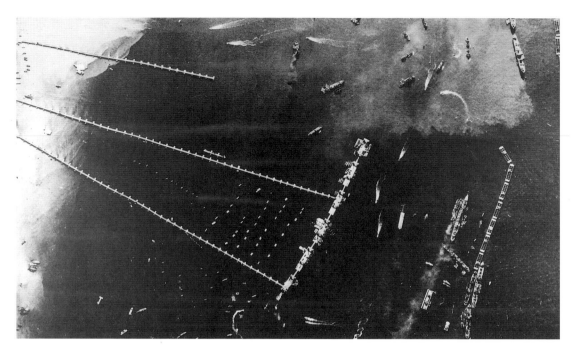

The capture of ports in the operational zone had been planned for, but it seemed probable that the Germans would have mined or destroyed them before the Allies could take them. Thus, the control of small but intact fishing harbours along the coast was very welcome.

One of them, PORT-EN-BESSIN, situated where the American and British operational zones met, was taken by a Royal Marine Commando unit on the night of 6th/7th June. From the 8th, it enabled a daily average of 1,000 tonnes of supplies to be handled, a figure greatly in excess of what was handled in peacetime.

Another important seizure was that of COURSEULLES, in the Canadian JUNO sector, to the east of Arromanches. Theoretically, this port should have been able to handle more than PORT-EN-BESSIN. Unfortunately, due as much to the neglect of maintenance in past years as to the destruction caused by the Germans, it proved impossible to improve its handling capacity and from the 8th of June it was only capable of dealing with 1,000 tonnes per day.

Other small Normandy ports, CARENTAN, GRANDCAMP, ISIGNY, BARFLEUR, and ST. VAAST contributed their modest share to the unloading of coastal shipping, although at low tide, they were mostly useless.
Grandcamp and Isigny, restored to service, received their first cargoes on 23rd June, St. Vaast on 9th July, and Carentan and Barfleur on 23rd July.

During July, given the danger of insufficient unloading capacity (i.e. 17,000 tonnes per day). it was decided to expand as far as possible the handling capacity of these small ports. It was estimated that Carentan and

Barfleur could, at full stretch, discharge, respectively, each day, 4,000 and 2,500 tonnes. The necessary dredging and infrastructure improvements began, but difficulties followed, one after another. So, Carentan was abandoned, after having worked for only from 23rd to 31st July.

After mid-October, at the latest, all these ports ceased to operate.

Unfortunately, at the first light of the 19th June, all this fine planning and all the effort spent to ensure a continuous flow of reinforcements were brought to naught by a storm of Force 6 to 7, of a severity unknown in those parts for a very long time . Beginning with a stiff breeze from the north-east, the storm raged for three days, causing considerable damage and sowing chaos along the Normandy coast. From the beginning of the storm, unloading operations were interrupted.

Certainly, this storm was not a surprise, because the planners had estimated that between May and September, stormy weather could occur for four successive days each month. Consequently, it had been planned to increase the daily rate of unloading by 30% as from D-day +4. What was more surprising, was the sheer strength of the storm; some said that nothing like it had been seen for forty years.

The storm died out on 22nd June, and from the 23rd, the DUKWs were again able to resume unloading operations.

On the American side, the harbour of St. Laurent was far from being completed and was very vulnerable. So as to facilitate beaching, the Americans had left additional gaps in the breakwater. Through these gaps, the storm raged to cause irreparable damage. The sole jettyhead to be in position in Mulberry A was destroyed by a group of 16 LCTs seeking shelter but only succeeding in colliding with the jettyhead.

In addition, it appears that the Americans had taken less care than the British in placing and fixing the elements of the artificial harbour. The scuttled ships were not sufficiently close together and the Phoenix caissons were sunk in water which was too deep and so were quickly submerged by waves breaking over them. In addition, the Americans were over-optimistic regarding the need for anchoring, whilst the British had doubled the number of all their anchors.

At Arromanches, the artificial harbour withstood valiantly the force of the storm. Further advanced in its construction than Mulberry A, it had been protected by Phœnix caissons and by the Calvados Bank, a rocky area offshore which gave protection from bottom swell.

■ ■ ■ BOTH WELCOME AND UNPLEASANT SURPRISES

That did not prevent some destruction, the shifting of the position of several caissons and a large number of craft being swept on to the shore (320 LCTs and numerous other craft). Everywhere, the rows of bombardons lost their anchors and, when they did not collide with and sink the Phœnix caissons, ended up on the beaches.

At Utah beach and at the other beaches, half the smaller flat-bottomed craft were unusable for 36 to 48 hours.

In the USA, during WW2, Major Ruppenthal stated that this storm was not among the most severe known to occur in the Channel, and that the weather conditions would prevent the use of the artificial harbours during the winter. He recalled that General Eisenhower, when faced with the extent of the storm damage, stressed the urgency of taking Cherbourg.

For Admiral Kirk, if the storm had highlighted the weaknesses of the Mulberries, it had also demonstrated the importance of the Gooseberries, which provided a relatively sheltered area for the smaller craft, thus facilitating their unloading.

This storm risked prejudicing the results of the previous weeks.

At Mulberry A, on 19th June, when the storm began, about half of the unloading objectives had been achieved. The unloading, in the American Sector of 8,300 tonnes of supplies, 3,000 vehicles and 17,750 men had taken place, From the next day, after the storm, the figures fell to only 1,000 tonnes, 738 vehicles and 3,300 men. Some types of ammunition began to run short at a time when the VIIth Corps started to launch its attack on

■ Arromanches after the storm of 19th June 1944

■ Arromanches today

■ The storm of the 19th June 1944 at Arromanches.

Cherbourg. In addition, the 1st U.S. Army decided to beach 8 ships containing munitions and gave orders to the unloading units to give priority to munitions and petrol.

Little by little, Mulberry B was able to resume its operations. During the storm, the unloading of ammunition was hindered; however as early as the 22nd of June, 1,200 of the 1,500 tonnes required by the British troops had been successfully unloaded.

In Normandy, after this great storm, which shattered both the hopes and plans of the Allies, just as it had devastated shipping (more than 800 vessels were blown on to the shore), all the harbour elements that were in the course of being towed across the Channel on the 19th were sunk. Those which arrived on the 20th and 21st were severely damaged. The British and Americans had to get to work again . As it was thought that Cherbourg was about to fall, Mulberry A was abandoned, whereas it could have been repaired in a few weeks. The destruction of Phoenix caissons was catastrophic. Twenty of the thirty caissons had been smashed by the force of the storm. Those that could be recovered were sent to Mulberry B. The remaining Phoenix units were to assist the unloading of the ships that were driven ashore during subsequent days. Only the shelter-jetty built of caissons was able to continue to offer shelter to the smaller landing craft. However, on 23rd June, unloading with DUKWs and ferries resumed and 10,000 tonnes reached land.

Later, Mulberry B was equipped with seven berthing quays on stilts, completing a central quay which now measured 750m. On 19th June, this work was completed. The east LST quay was the last to enter into service on the 17th of July.

■ The storm of the 19th June 1944 at Arromanches

Protected by the Gooseberries, the various beaches continued to contribute to resupplying the troops, either by transferring the supplies on to DUKWs or by beaching coasters. At Omaha, it was realised that the rocks were friable and a fleet of bulldozers set about making the beach suitable for the simultaneous beaching of a large number of ships which unloaded their cargoes directly on to lorries.

At the beginning of August, Supreme Allied Headquarters decided to continue using the artificial harbour at Arromanches for as long as the weather would allow, and therefore rejected the British Headquarters proposal to use Cherbourg as soon as Brest was liberated. At the same time, it was decided to strengthen the harbour, in particular, by increasing the number of Phoenix caissons, so that it could function during the winter.

In September, General GALE, of SHAEF, underlined the urgency of this reinforcement programme, noting that though Cherbourg had been taken two months earlier, it had not been possible to provide a berth for a single Liberty Ship (LIBERTY SHIPS were capable of transporting over 7,000 tonnes of supplies, i.e., three times the capacity of the largest coasters). With the capture of Antwerp on 4th September and Le Havre on the 12th, the lack of port facilities for unloading was about to come to an end. Moreover, the measures needed to make the harbour safe for use in winter were costly and the deterioration of the roads in the hinterland required considerable repair works.

By mid-October, Montgomery's 21st Army Group was anxious to recover its personnel and mobile port equipment which remained at Arromanches, so as to be able to re-equip the Belgian ports recently liberated (save for Antwerp which was only able to reopen on 26th November). At this time, Mulberry B was only being used to discharge American Liberty Ships and for the transit of reserve supplies. The deterioration of the roads in the hinterland, coupled with the low capacity of the railway which served a port some 20km from there, caused the reconsideration of earlier decisions and, on the 16th of October, a SHAEF conference ordered the abandonment of the preparations for making the harbour suitable for winter operations and transferred the spare Phoenix and various other items to Le Havre, operational from the 9th October.

Nevertheless, the unloading of supplies continued until the 31st of the month and torpedo boats went on using the harbour for as long as the weather allowed.

Everything that could be removed was recovered, with the exception of one floating jetty reserved for U.S. ships and which operated until the 19th November, when Omaha ceased unloading operations. The harbour was then abandoned.

THREE REASONS PREVAILED FOR THE CLOSURE OF ARROMANCHES :

The opening of Belgian and Dutch ports which were much closer to the battle zone in Montgomery's 21st Army and also to Nancy, where the American 3rd Army had its advanced base.

In addition, for supplies unloaded in Normandy, the rail links to the East could only handle 10,000 tonnes per day (against 20,000 tonnes unloaded), hence the need to use a large fleet of lorries.

The use of Antwerp considerably reduced the distance between the logistical bases and the front lines and did away with the complicated logistical system known as RED BALL EXPRESS (this system consisted of reserving certain roads for military traffic. These one-way roads, starting from the Normandy beaches, went via Chartres, whence one route passed through Soissons and the other through Arcis-sur-Aube. Supplies passed over these roads in a continuous stream, day and night).

The deterioration of the roads in Arromanches and the surrounding area. This deterioration took place because of the incessant traffic over four months. It had been a constant worry for those responsible for the area and the steps taken had proved inadequate, given the number of vehicles in circulation.

The silting up of the Arromanches harbour , where sandbanks appeared here and there whilst at other points, the structures were settling into the sea bed, causing unforeseeable movements of the breakwaters and the quays.

Designed to operate only during the ninety days of summer, the harbour had not only stood up to use for a much longer time, but its contribution to supplying the troops had been considerable.

A BALANCE SHEET

During the first week of the invasion, the daily average of arrivals of shipping carrying equipment and supplies for the forces which had landed was as follows :

25 Liberty Ships
38 Coasters
9 Troop transports
40 LSTs (tank landing ships)
75 LCTs (tank landing craft)
20 LCIs (infantry landing craft)

In detail, these deliveries to the beaches are broken down as follows :

Quantities landed on the British beaches :

From 6th to 19th June, the British beaches allowed the unloading within the shelter of the Gooseberries of: 120,729 tonnes, 50,400 vehicles and 286,586 men. The Courseulles Gooseberry was the most efficient of the three British ones. It allowed the average daily unloading of 1,028 tonnes and was used for the evacuation of the wounded to ships anchored 5 nautical miles offshore.

Quantities landed at Arromanches, Mulberry B :

Designed for unloading 6,000 tonnes of equipment per day as from the 20th June, Mulberry B surpassed this figure by handling an average of 6,765 tonnes for three months; i.e., 48% of the total tonnage unloaded for the benefit of the British forces. At the end of the second week of August, more than 10,000 vehicles had passed over the Arromanches quays, i.e., 5.5% of the British vehicles landed in France. And 120,000 men had landed there (Statistics available from the British are much more sparse than those available from the Americans, where the daily numbers of troops landed and supplies handled were known from day to day).

The following figures offer an insight into the great acheivement at Arromanches: on the central quay alone, 239,000 tonnes of supplies were unloaded, a further 290,000 tonnes being directly brought to shore by the DUKWs (amphibious vehicles), throughout the duration of the harbour's operations (up to the 19th of November 1944). By late October 1944, 220,000 men and 39,000 vehicles had landed on the east LST quay. At this point in time, Arromanches had facilitated the landing of 20% of troops, 15% of vehicles and 25% of supplies.

Without the artificial harbours, the Allied armies, lacking regular resupplies, would have been unable to exploit fully those small signs of weakness or indecision displayed by the enemy. It is not inconceivable that, in the absence of artifical harbours, the Battle of Normandy might not have been won by the Allies.

The harbours enabled the allied troops to profit from a supply system which surpassed anything that the Germans were able to achieve in Normandy.

Without the harbours, no Army commander would have taken the decision to invade. The failure at Dieppe had demonstrated the vital necessity of having a port or harbour available from the very start of the battle; it was therefore clear to the senior Allied commanders that the Germans would strongly defend the Channel ports and that these, even when once captured, would be rendered useless for many weeks by the destruction wreaked beforehand. This is indeed what happened at Cherbourg, in Brittany and in the Pas-de-Calais.

CONCLUSION

The technical reasons for the success of the landings are many :
- the perfect secrecy maintained and the efficacy of the deception plan known as Operation Fortitude,
- mastery of the air and sea,
- the volume and accuracy of the intelligence gained,
- the role of the French Resistance,
- the wise choice of location for the invasion,
- the sheer magnitude of the operation the Atlantic Wall was not so much smashed as overwhelmed.

Despite the capture of Antwerp on 4th September, it was impossible to use it as a logistical base until the 28th November, a day on which the seizure of Walcheren finally opened up access to this large port. Thus, during this vital period of the campaign, the supply lines, specially for the Americans, were reliant on Cherbourg, Arromanches and the Normandy beaches.

At Christmas 1944, the dismantling of Arromanches began. The bridging units would be used to replace bridges which had been destroyed, so making savings of the Bailey bridges which had been allocated to such use. Some refloated caissons would replace sections of dyke on Walcheren which had been damaged by Allied bombing.

After the surrender of Germany, the British Army handed over to the French 183 steel sections of floating jetties which, from 1945 to 1948, permitted the rebuilding of about 60 large civil engineering structures.

The construction, in England, of the massive and bulky Mulberry elements, their concealment from enemy intelligence, their transportation across the Channel to the beaches, their careful placing in position and the way in which those at Arromanches withstood the storms, made the artificial ports one of the major and essential features of the Normandy landings. 45,000 men worked for eight months to build this floating structure which, once complete weighed a total of nearly one million tonnes. The construction of the first 147 caissons during this period required somme 660,000 tonnes of concrete and 31,000 tonnes of steel. A further 60,000 tonnes of steel were used to build the floating quays and their roadways. The only genuine floating roadways (supported by concrete floaters), together with their 8 access ramps, also « absorbed » 30,000 tonnes of steel and concrete. They participated in supporting over a million Allied troops.

The construction of the Mulberries was probably the greatest military engineering enterprise undertaken since the Persian armies crossed over the Bosphorous, on a pontoon bridge, in B.C. 480.

The D-Day Museum

The permanent exhibition of the landings was created in 1953 and officially inaugurated on 5th June 1954 by the then President of the Republic, Monsieur René COTY.

After having been managed by the D-Day Landing Committee since its creation, the museum is now run by the *Groupement d'Intérêt Public d'Arromanches*.

The museum stands on the very site of the artificial harbour, which remains can still be seen a few hundred yards offshore.

Your museum visit ...

The models

Whilst the nearby panoramic window offers views out to sea and towards the ruins of « Mulberry B », our guide will explain the port's construction and operations in 1944 via small-scale models. Some of them are animated, showing precise tidal movements and illustrating the modernity of these ingenious port facilities.

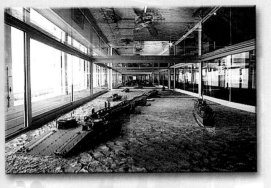

The diorama (7 minutes)

For seven minutes, relive the intense emotion of the night before D-Day by viewing this projection commentated by Mr Raymond Triboulet, former Minister to Charles de Gaulle and first Sub-Prefect of liberated France. The diorama is available in French, English, German, Dutch, Italian and Spanish.

The galleries

In the museum's galleries, you will discover the twelve nations that took part in the D-Day landings as well as uniforms and items belonging to some of the soldiers. The museum also has its own gift shop offering a wide range of products and souvenirs.

The cinema (15 minutes)

A 15 minute film from the archives, produced by the British Admiralty and illustrating the main stages in the harbour's construction and its use, is your visit's finishing touch. For foreign visitors, the film is shown in: English, German, Dutch, Italian, Spanish, Japanese, Czech and Chinese.